RAUL MORALES

Cyber Defense Made Simple: Your Accessible Guide

To the business builders,
I dedicate this book to you. You are the ones who create jobs, drive
innovation, and make the world a better place. Cybersecurity is
essential for the success of your business.
I hope this book helps you build a more secure future.

Contents

Foreword

Cybersecurity is a critical issue for businesses of all sizes. In today's digital world, businesses are constantly under threat from cyber attacks. These attacks can range from simple phishing emails to sophisticated data breaches.

The consequences of a cyber attack can be devastating for a business. Financial losses, damage to reputation, and legal liability are just a few of the potential consequences.

That's why it's so important for businesses to have a comprehensive cybersecurity strategy in place. This strategy should include a risk assessment, policies and procedures, employee training, and an incident response plan.

This book is designed to help non-technical executives understand cybersecurity and develop a comprehensive cybersecurity strategy for their businesses.

The book is divided into 14 chapters. Each chapter covers a different aspect of cybersecurity, such as:
  * Types of cyber attacks
  * Developing a cybersecurity strategy
  * Cybersecurity standards and regulations
  * Securing cloud-based applications and services

* Protecting mobile devices
* Securing the Internet of Things (IoT)
* Cybersecurity insurance
* Recruiting cybersecurity talent
* Managing third-party cybersecurity risks
* Responding to cybersecurity incidents
* Cybersecurity for remote work
* Future trends in cybersecurity
* Conclusion

The book uses real-world examples to illustrate the importance of cybersecurity and the potential consequences of ignoring it.

By reading this book, non-technical executives will gain a better understanding of cybersecurity and be able to develop a comprehensive cybersecurity strategy for their businesses.

Acknowledgement

I would like to take a moment to express my heartfelt appreciation to the individuals who have contributed to the creation of this book on cybersecurity.

First and foremost, I am immensely grateful to my wife, I Wen, for her unwavering love, support, and understanding throughout the entire writing process. Your encouragement and belief in me have been instrumental in bringing this book to fruition.

I would also like to extend my sincere gratitude to my dedicated team of test readers, Sofia, Mario,Patricia,Romny,Marta and Nelson. Your valuable feedback, meticulous attention to detail, and insightful suggestions have significantly enhanced the quality and clarity of the content. Your commitment and dedication have been invaluable in shaping this book into its final form.

Furthermore, I would like to acknowledge the numerous individuals, mentors, and colleagues who have shared their knowledge and expertise in the field of cybersecurity. Your insights and guidance have been invaluable sources of inspiration and have helped shape the concepts discussed within this book.

Finally, I would like to express my gratitude to the readers of this book. It is my hope that the information and insights shared within these pages will empower you to navigate the intricate world of cybersecurity with confidence and clarity.

Thank you all for your unwavering support and contributions.

With deepest appreciation,
  Raul Morales

1

Chapter 1: Introduction

In today's interconnected world, where technology plays a pivotal role in nearly every aspect of our lives, the importance of cybersecurity cannot be overstated. As a non-technical executive, you may have heard the term "cybersecurity" thrown around, but what does it really mean? And why should it matter to you and your organization?

1.1 The Growing Importance of Cybersecurity

Cybersecurity has become a critical concern for businesses of all sizes and industries. The digital landscape is teeming with threats, and the consequences of a successful cyber attack can be devastating. Cybersecurity is important for businesses because it protects their data, systems, and operations from unauthorized access, use, disclosure, disruption, modification, or destruction. Cybersecurity also protects businesses from financial losses, reputational damage, and legal liability.

The cost of cyber attacks is increasing. In 2021, the global cost of cyber attacks was estimated to be $6 trillion. This number is expected to grow in the coming years.

Take, for example, the case of Equifax, one of the largest credit reporting agencies. In 2017, Equifax suffered a massive data breach, compromising the personal information of approximately 147 million people. The fallout from this breach was staggering, resulting in a loss of customer trust, legal liabilities, regulatory fines, and significant financial losses. Equifax's market value plummeted by billions of dollars in the aftermath of the incident.

This is just one example among many that highlight the potential consequences of ignoring cybersecurity. The truth is, no organization is immune to cyber threats. Whether you're a multinational corporation or a small startup, cybercriminals see value in your data and will exploit any vulnerability they can find. It's not a matter of "if" but "when" your organization will be targeted.

1.2 Cybersecurity as a Business Issue

Many executives mistakenly believe that cybersecurity is solely a technical problem that falls under the purview of IT departments. However, this mindset is outdated and dangerous. Cybersecurity is, first and foremost, a business issue that requires the attention and involvement of the entire organization, from the C-suite to every employee.

Cybersecurity is everyone's responsibility. However, the responsibility for cybersecurity ultimately falls to the business's executive team. Executives are responsible for setting cybersecurity policies and procedures, allocating resources for cybersecurity, and ensuring that cybersecurity is a priority for the business.

Consider the case of Target, a major retail chain. In 2013, Target fell victim to a cyber attack that compromised the credit card information of over 40 million customers. The breach occurred through a third-party HVAC contractor, highlighting the interconnectedness of supply chains and the need for holistic cybersecurity measures. Target's failure to adequately assess and manage third-party risks resulted in significant financial losses and a damaged reputation.

The Target breach demonstrates that cybersecurity is not just about firewalls, encryption, and technical jargon. It's about understanding the business risks associated with cyber threats and implementing a comprehensive strategy to mitigate those risks. As a non-technical executive, your role is crucial in ensuring that your organization adopts a proactive and integrated approach to cybersecurity.

1.3 The Cost of Cyber Attacks

Beyond the immediate financial losses incurred by cyber attacks, there are other significant costs that organizations must bear. One such cost is the damage to reputation. In today's hyper connected world, news spreads like wildfire, and a single cybersecurity incident can tarnish your organization's image for years to come. Customers, partners, and investors may lose trust in your ability to protect their sensitive information, leading to a decline in business opportunities and financial performance.

Legal liabilities are another consequence of cyber attacks. In recent years, there has been a surge in data protection regulations worldwide, such as the European Union's General Data Protection Regulation (GDPR) and the California Consumer Privacy Act (CCPA). Noncompliance with these regulations can result in severe fines and legal actions. For instance, British Airways was fined £20 million ($27 million) by the UK's Information Commissioner's Office (ICO) for failing to protect customer data during a 2018 breach.

Furthermore, the costs associated with incident response, remediation, and recovery can be astronomical. Organizations often need to hire specialized cybersecurity firms, conduct forensic investigations, implement new security measures, and provide identity theft protection services to affected individuals. These expenses can quickly add up, further straining the organization's resources.

1.4 The Human Factor

While sophisticated technologies and complex algorithms are often associated with cybersecurity, it is important to recognize that humans are a crucial part of the equation. Employees, including executives, can either be the strongest line of defense or the weakest link in an organization's cybersecurity posture.

Phishing attacks, for example, are a prevalent method used by cybercriminals to gain unauthorized access to systems and sensitive information. These attacks often involve deceiving employees into clicking on malicious links or providing their login credentials. In 2020, amidst the COVID-19 pandemic, there was a surge in phishing attacks targeting remote workers who were vulnerable due to the sudden shift to remote work and potential lack of security awareness.

To mitigate such risks, organizations must invest in cybersecurity education and awareness programs. As a non-technical executive, it is imperative that you understand the basics of cybersecurity and the role you play in promoting a culture of security within your organization. By leading by example and prioritizing cybersecurity, you can foster a vigilant and proactive mindset among your employees.

1.5 The Scope of This Book

In this book, we aim to equip non-technical executives like yourself with the knowledge and understanding needed to navigate the complex world of cybersecurity. We will demystify technical jargon and explain cybersecurity concepts in a language that is accessible and relevant to your role.

Over the course of the following chapters, we will explore various aspects of cybersecurity and provide practical guidance on how to protect your organization effectively. We will cover topics such as the different types of cybersecurity threats, developing a cybersecurity strategy, compliance with regulations, securing cloud-based applications and services, protecting mobile devices, securing the Internet of Things (IoT), cybersecurity insurance, recruiting cybersecurity talent, managing third-party risks, responding to incidents, addressing cybersecurity challenges in remote work environments, and exploring future trends in cybersecurity.

By the end of this book, you will have a solid foundation in cybersecurity, enabling you to make informed decisions and take proactive measures to safeguard your organization. Remember, cybersecurity is not an isolated responsibility but a collective effort that requires ongoing vigilance and commitment from every member of your organization.

Stay tuned as we embark on this cybersecurity journey together, empowering you to navigate the digital landscape with confidence and resilience.

2

Chapter 2: Types of Cybersecurity Threats

In this chapter, we will explore the different types of cyberse-curity threats that businesses face in today's digital landscape. Understanding these threats is crucial for non-technical execu-tives like yourself, as it enables you to identify vulnerabilities and take appropriate measures to protect your organization.

The landscape where business are made is full of threats, it is our responsibility to know about them lest we become their prey

2.1 Malware: The Silent Intruder

Malware, short for malicious software, refers to any software designed to harm or exploit computer systems, networks, or users. It is one of the most common and pervasive cybersecurity threats faced by organizations worldwide. Malware can take various forms, including viruses, worms, Trojans, ransomware, and spyware.

Viruses are programs that replicate themselves and infect other files or systems. They can cause damage by corrupting or destroying data, disrupting system functionality, or spreading to other connected devices. A famous example is the ILOVEYOU virus, which spread through email attachments in 2000, causing widespread damage by overwriting files on infected machines.

Worms, on the other hand, are standalone programs that can spread across networks without human intervention. They exploit vulnerabilities in operating systems or network protocols to replicate and infect other devices. The WannaCry ransomware attack in 2017 utilized a worm to rapidly infect vulnerable systems, causing significant disruptions in healthcare, transportation, and other sectors.

Trojans, named after the Trojan horse from Greek mythology, appear harmless or useful but contain hidden malicious functionalities. They often trick users into installing them, giving cybercriminals unauthorized access to the system. A well-known example is the Zeus Trojan, which targeted online banking users, stealing their login credentials and financial information.

Ransomware has gained notoriety in recent years, where cybercriminals encrypt victims' files and demand a ransom payment in exchange for the decryption key. The WannaCry attack mentioned earlier was a significant ransomware incident, causing widespread chaos and financial losses. The Colonial Pipeline ransomware attack in 2021 also made headlines, leading to fuel shortages and highlighting the critical infrastructure risks posed by ransomware.

Spyware, as the name suggests, is designed to gather information stealthily from an infected device. It can monitor user activities, capture sensitive information, and transmit it to malicious actors. Mobile spyware applications that secretly track a user's location, messages, and calls are a growing concern in the era of smartphones.

Protecting against malware requires a multi-layered approach, including strong antivirus and anti malware software, regular updates and patches, employee education on safe online practices, and robust backup and recovery mechanisms.

2.2 Phishing: The Art of Deception

Phishing attacks are a type of social engineering attack in which cybercriminals masquerade as trustworthy entities to trick individuals into divulging sensitive information or performing harmful actions. Phishing attacks typically occur through email, but they can also happen through other communication channels such as phone calls or text messages.

Phishing emails often mimic legitimate organizations or individuals, using convincing logos, email addresses, and content to deceive recipients. They employ psychological tactics to create a sense of urgency, fear, or curiosity, compelling users to click on malicious links or provide confidential information like usernames, passwords, or financial details.

In 2020, the COVID-19 pandemic became a fertile ground for phishing attacks. Cybercriminals exploited the fear and uncertainty surrounding the pandemic by sending phishing emails impersonating health organizations, government agencies, and relief organizations. These emails claimed to provide essential information or assistance related to the pandemic, tricking users into clicking on malicious links or downloading infected attachments.

Spear phishing is a more targeted form of phishing that focuses on specific individuals or organizations. Attackers gather detailed information about their targets, such as their roles, interests, or social connections, to personalize their phishing attempts and increase their chances of success. Executive-level employees are often prime targets for spear phishing due to their access to sensitive information and authority within the organization.

To defend against phishing attacks, organizations must educate their employees about common phishing techniques and provide guidelines on how to spot and report suspicious emails. Implementing robust email filtering systems, multi-factor authentication, and secure communication protocols can also significantly reduce the risk of falling victim to phishing attacks.

2.3 Ransomware: Holding Data Hostage

Ransomware attacks have become increasingly prevalent and disruptive in recent years. These attacks involve encrypting an organization's files or systems, making them inaccessible until a ransom is paid. Ransomware is typically delivered through phishing emails, malicious attachments, or exploiting vulnerabilities in software or systems.

Once infected, the victim receives a ransom demand, often accompanied by threats of permanent data loss or public exposure of sensitive information. The ransom is usually demanded in cryptocurrencies like Bitcoin, which provide a certain level of anonymity for the attackers.

The impact of ransomware attacks can be severe. In 2021, the Colonial Pipeline, one of the largest fuel pipelines in the United States, fell victim to a ransomware attack. The attack forced the pipeline's temporary shutdown, leading to fuel shortages and significant disruptions across the East Coast. The incident highlighted the vulnerabilities of critical infrastructure to ransomware attacks and the potential cascading effects on daily life.

Another notable ransomware incident involved the global shipping company Maersk in 2017. The NotPetya ransomware infected Maersk's IT systems, causing widespread disruptions in their operations. The company had to rebuild its entire IT infrastructure from scratch, resulting in an estimated financial loss of $300 million.

To protect against ransomware attacks, organizations should

implement a defense-in-depth strategy, including regular backups of critical data, network segmentation to limit the impact of an attack, robust patch management processes, and employee training on safe computing practices. It is essential to have an incident response plan in place to minimize the damage and swiftly recover from an attack.

2.4 Supply Chain Attacks: Breaking the Weakest Link

Supply chain attacks have gained significant attention in recent years as cybercriminals have recognized the potential to exploit vulnerabilities in an organization's supply chain to infiltrate their targets. A supply chain attack involves compromising a trusted supplier or vendor to gain unauthorized access to the target organization's systems or data.

The SolarWinds supply chain attack in 2020 sent shockwaves across the cybersecurity landscape. Cybercriminals breached the software development infrastructure of SolarWinds, a leading IT management software provider, and injected malicious code into their software updates. As a result, approximately 18,000 SolarWinds customers unknowingly installed the compromised updates, granting the attackers access to their networks. The attack affected numerous government agencies, technology companies, and other organizations worldwide.

Supply chain attacks can be highly effective because they exploit the trust that organizations place in their suppliers and vendors. Cybercriminals often target smaller or less secure organizations in the supply chain to gain a foothold and then use that access to move laterally to higher-value targets.

To mitigate supply chain risks, organizations should implement a robust vendor management program that includes due diligence, regular security assessments, and contractual requirements for cybersecurity measures. It is crucial to verify the security practices of suppliers and establish strong communication channels to promptly address any potential vulnerabilities or incidents.

2.5 Zero-day Exploits: Unseen Vulnerabilities

Zero-day exploits refer to vulnerabilities in software or systems that are unknown to the vendor and, therefore, have no patches or fixes available. Cybercriminals capitalize on these vulnerabilities to gain unauthorized access to systems, steal sensitive data, or carry out other malicious activities.

The term "zero-day" signifies that organizations have zero days to protect themselves before an attack occurs. When a zero-day vulnerability is discovered and exploited, it can have devastating consequences, as organizations have no time to prepare or implement countermeasures.

In 2021, the Microsoft Exchange Server zero-day vulnerabilities known as ProxyLogon were exploited by advanced threat actors. These vulnerabilities allowed attackers to gain persistent access to Exchange Server environments, leading to unauthorized data access, malware deployment, and further compromise of the affected systems.

To defend against zero-day exploits, organizations should implement a proactive approach to security, including regular software updates, patch management processes, and intrusion detection and prevention systems. Maintaining strong relationships with software vendors and staying informed about emerging threats and vulnerabilities is also essential to respond effectively to zero-day exploits when they are discovered.

In this chapter, we explored several types of cybersecurity threats that organizations face in today's digital landscape. From malware and phishing attacks to ransomware, supply chain attacks, and zero-day exploits, it is clear that the threat landscape is constantly evolving and becoming increasingly sophisticated.

As a non-technical executive, it is crucial to be aware of these threats and their potential impact on your organization. By understanding the nature of these threats, you can better allocate resources, prioritize security initiatives, and promote a culture of cybersecurity within your organization.

3

Chapter 3: Developing a Cybersecurity Strategy

In this chapter, we will explore the steps involved in developing a comprehensive cybersecurity strategy for your organization. A well-defined cybersecurity strategy is essential for protecting your business from cyber threats and minimizing the potential impact of security incidents. By following these steps, non-technical executives can play a vital role in safeguarding their organizations' digital assets.

Creating a strategy is pivotal for the company's survival

3.1 Step 1: Conducting a Risk Assessment

Before developing a cybersecurity strategy, it is crucial to assess your organization's current security posture and identify potential risks and vulnerabilities. A risk assessment helps you understand the specific threats that your organization faces and prioritize your security efforts.

Start by identifying the critical assets and data that your organization needs to protect. This can include customer information, intellectual property, financial data, or any other sensitive information. Consider the potential impact of a security breach on these assets, including financial losses, reputational damage, regulatory penalties, and legal liabilities.

Next, evaluate the existing security controls and practices in place. This includes assessing your network infrastructure, access controls, incident response capabilities, employee awareness and training programs, and any other security measures. Identify any gaps or weaknesses that need to be addressed.

Consider the external factors that can pose a risk to your organization, such as the current threat landscape, industry-specific risks, regulatory requirements, and emerging technologies. Stay updated on the latest cybersecurity trends, threat intelligence reports, and best practices relevant to your industry.

A real-world example of the importance of risk assessment is the Equifax data breach in 2017. Equifax, one of the largest credit reporting agencies, experienced a massive data breach that exposed sensitive information of over 143 million individuals. The breach was a result of multiple security vulnerabilities and failures, including outdated software, unpatched systems, and poor security practices. A thorough risk assessment could have helped identify these vulnerabilities and prevent the breach.

3.2 Step 2: Developing Policies and Procedures

Once you have identified the risks and vulnerabilities, it is essential to establish clear policies and procedures to mitigate those risks and guide employees in their cybersecurity practices. Policies and procedures provide a framework for consistent security practices across the organization and ensure that employees understand their roles and responsibilities in maintaining security.

Develop an acceptable use policy that outlines the acceptable and prohibited uses of organizational resources, including computers, networks, and software. This policy should address issues such as password management, social media usage, and downloading of unauthorized software.

Create an incident response plan that outlines the steps to be taken in the event of a security incident. This plan should include roles and responsibilities, communication protocols, escalation procedures, and steps for containment, eradication, and recovery.

Consider creating a data classification policy that defines different levels of sensitivity for data and specifies the appropriate security controls and access rights for each level. This policy helps ensure that sensitive information is adequately protected based on its value and potential impact if compromised.

Employee awareness and training programs are vital for ensuring that employees understand the organization's cybersecurity policies and procedures. Conduct regular training sessions on topics such as password security, phishing awareness, safe browsing practices, and data protection. Make cybersecurity training an ongoing process to keep employees informed about evolving threats and best practices.

An example of the importance of policies and procedures is the Target data breach in 2013. Attackers gained access to Target's network through a third-party vendor and installed malware on the point-of-sale systems. The breach resulted in the theft of credit card information of millions of customers. Target's incident response plan was inadequate, and the organization lacked proper network segmentation and access controls. Implementing strong policies and procedures could have helped prevent or mitigate the impact of the breach.

3.3 Step 3: Training Employees

Employees play a critical role in maintaining the security of an organization's digital assets. Therefore, it is essential to provide comprehensive cybersecurity training to all employees, regardless of their technical expertise. Training programs should focus on raising awareness about common cyber threats and providing guidance on best practices for mitigating those threats.

Start by educating employees about the various types of cyber threats they may encounter, such as phishing emails, social engineering, malware, and ransomware. Use real-world examples and case studies to demonstrate the potential consequences of falling victim to these threats.

Train employees on how to recognize and respond to phishing attempts. Teach them to scrutinize email senders, avoid clicking on suspicious links or downloading attachments from unknown sources, and report any suspicious activity to the appropriate channels.

Emphasize the importance of strong passwords and proper password management. Encourage employees to use complex passwords, enable multi-factor authentication, and avoid reusing passwords across different accounts.

Promote safe browsing habits and caution when accessing websites, especially those with unknown or suspicious origins. Teach employees about the dangers of visiting malicious websites, downloading unauthorized software, or clicking on pop-up ads.

Highlight the importance of keeping software and systems up to date. Encourage employees to promptly install software updates and patches to mitigate the risk of known vulnerabilities being exploited.

Provide guidance on the secure use of mobile devices, such as smartphones and tablets. Teach employees to enable passcodes, use encryption, and avoid connecting to unsecured Wi-Fi networks.

Regularly reinforce cybersecurity training through newsletters, posters, and reminders. Consider conducting simulated phishing campaigns to test employees' awareness and provide feedback on areas that need improvement.

One notable example of the importance of employee training is the WannaCry ransomware attack in 2017. The ransomware spread rapidly across the globe, affecting organizations in various industries. The attack exploited a vulnerability in the Windows operating system for which a patch had been available for several months. Many organizations fell victim to WannaCry because their employees were not trained to recognize and respond to phishing emails or to promptly install software updates.

3.4 Step 4: Creating an Incident Response Plan

Despite the best preventive measures, no organization is entirely immune to cybersecurity incidents. Therefore, it is crucial to have an incident response plan in place to minimize the impact of a security breach and facilitate a swift and effective response.

An incident response plan outlines the steps to be taken when a security incident occurs, ensuring a coordinated and organized approach. The plan should define roles and responsibilities for incident response team members, establish communication protocols, and outline the technical and procedural steps to be followed.

Establish a clear chain of command and identify individuals who will be responsible for making critical decisions during an incident. This includes designating a response team leader and defining the roles of other team members, such as technical experts, legal advisors, and public relations representatives.

Develop a communication plan that specifies how internal and external stakeholders will be notified during an incident. This includes employees, customers, partners, regulators, and law enforcement agencies. Determine the appropriate channels for communication, such as email, internal messaging systems, or dedicated incident response platforms.

Define the technical steps to be taken during an incident, such as isolating affected systems, collecting evidence, analyzing the impact, and restoring normal operations. This may involve engaging the organization's IT team or external cybersecurity experts for assistance.

Establish relationships with external resources that can provide support during a security incident, such as forensic investigators, legal counsel specializing in cybersecurity, and public relations consultants. Having these relationships in place in advance can expedite the response and ensure that the organization receives the necessary expertise when needed.

Test and validate the incident response plan through tabletop exercises and simulations. These exercises help identify any gaps or weaknesses in the plan and allow the incident response team to practice their roles and responsibilities. Regularly update and refine the plan based on lessons learned from these exercises and real-world incidents.

An example of the importance of an incident response plan is the 2014 breach at Sony Pictures Entertainment. The attack resulted in the theft of sensitive data, including employee records, unreleased films, and executive emails. Sony's response to the breach was criticized for being disorganized and lacking a clear incident response plan. A well-defined plan would have enabled a more coordinated response and helped mitigate the impact of the breach.

3.5 Step 5: Ongoing Monitoring and Improvement

Cybersecurity is not a one-time effort but an ongoing process. Regular monitoring and continuous improvement are necessary to adapt to evolving threats and ensure the effectiveness of your cybersecurity strategy.

Implement a system for monitoring and analyzing security logs and events to detect any suspicious or anomalous activities. This can involve deploying security information and event management (SIEM) tools that collect and correlate data from various sources, such as firewalls, intrusion detection systems, and endpoint protection solutions.

Establish key performance indicators (KPIs) and metrics to measure the effectiveness of your cybersecurity strategy. This can include metrics related to incident response time, employee training completion rates, patch management effectiveness, and vulnerability remediation.

Regularly conduct vulnerability assessments and penetration testing to identify any weaknesses or vulnerabilities in your systems and infrastructure. These assessments can help you prioritize remediation efforts and ensure that security controls are functioning as intended.

Stay informed about the latest cybersecurity trends, emerging threats, and best practices through industry publications, security forums, and participation in relevant conferences and webinars. Consider joining industry-specific information sharing and analysis centers (ISACs) or collaborating with peer organizations to exchange threat intelligence and insights.

Encourage a culture of cybersecurity awareness and accountability throughout the organization. Foster a mindset where employees take ownership of their cybersecurity responsibilities and are encouraged to report any security concerns or incidents promptly.

Regularly review and update your cybersecurity policies, procedures, and training materials to reflect changes in technology, regulations, and industry standards. Engage relevant stakeholders, such as legal, compliance, and IT teams, to ensure that your cybersecurity efforts align with organizational objectives and comply with applicable laws and regulations.

An example of the importance of ongoing monitoring and improvement is the SolarWinds supply chain attack that came to light in late 2020. Advanced threat actors compromised SolarWinds' software update process and distributed a trojanized version of the Orion network monitoring software to thousands of organizations. The attack went undetected for several months, highlighting the need for robust monitoring and continuous improvement of security controls.

In conclusion, developing a comprehensive cybersecurity strategy is essential for protecting your organization's digital assets in today's threat landscape. By conducting a risk assessment, developing policies and procedures, training employees, creating an incident response plan, and implementing ongoing monitoring and improvement measures, non-technical executives can play a crucial role in ensuring the cybersecurity resilience of their organizations. In the next chapter, we will delve into the various cybersecurity standards and regulations that organizations need to comply with to enhance their security posture and protect their stakeholders' interests.

4

Chapter 4: Cybersecurity Standards and Regulations

In today's interconnected and digitized world, organizations face an increasing number of cybersecurity threats. To address these risks and protect sensitive data, businesses must comply with various cybersecurity standards and regulations. In this chapter, we will explore the importance of compliance, the potential consequences of noncompliance, and provide an overview of some key cybersecurity standards and regulations that non-technical executives should be aware of.

By researching and complying with regional standards you will expand the business reach of your company

4.1 The Importance of Compliance:

Compliance with cybersecurity standards and regulations is crucial for several reasons. First and foremost, it helps organizations establish a baseline level of security and protect sensitive information from unauthorized access, loss, or theft. Compliance also fosters trust among customers, partners, and stakeholders, demonstrating a commitment to safeguarding data and maintaining the integrity of business operations.

Moreover, compliance with cybersecurity standards can also provide legal and regulatory benefits. Many industries have specific requirements and guidelines to protect sensitive data and ensure privacy, such as the Health Insurance Portability and Accountability Act (HIPAA) for healthcare organizations or the Payment Card Industry Data Security Standard (PCI DSS) for businesses handling credit card information. Failure to comply with these regulations can result in severe penalties, fines, legal actions, and reputational damage.

4.2 Overview of Cybersecurity Standards and Regulations:

4.2.1 General Data Protection Regulation (GDPR):

The General Data Protection Regulation (GDPR) is a European Union (EU) regulation that sets guidelines for the collection, processing, and protection of personal data. It applies to organizations that handle the personal data of EU citizens, regardless of their geographical location. The GDPR emphasizes the principles of data minimization, purpose limitation, and consent, and grants individuals enhanced rights over their personal data. Non-compliance with the GDPR can result in fines of up to 4% of global annual revenue or €20 million, whichever is higher.

For example, in 2019, British Airways was fined £183 million ($230 million) by the UK Information Commissioner's Office

(ICO) for a data breach that exposed the personal information of approximately 500,000 customers. The fine was imposed under the GDPR for failing to implement adequate security measures to protect customer data.

4.2.2 California Consumer Privacy Act (CCPA):

The California Consumer Privacy Act (CCPA) is a state-level privacy law in the United States, granting California residents greater control over their personal information. The CCPA applies to businesses that meet specific criteria, including annual gross revenues above a certain threshold or processing a significant amount of personal data. It provides consumers with the right to know what personal information is being collected, the right to opt-out of the sale of their data, and the right to request the deletion of their data. Non-compliance with the CCPA can result in fines of up to $7,500 per violation.

An example of CCPA enforcement is the lawsuit against Zoom Video Communications in 2020. The video conferencing platform faced a class-action lawsuit for allegedly sharing user data with third-party platforms without proper disclosure, violating the CCPA's provisions.

4.2.3 ISO 27001:

ISO 27001 is an international standard for information security management systems (ISMS). It provides a framework for organizations to establish, implement, maintain, and continually improve their information security management processes. ISO 27001 encompasses various security controls and risk management practices, ensuring that organizations take a systematic approach to protect their information assets. Achieving ISO 27001 certification demonstrates a commitment to maintaining a robust information security posture.

For instance, Microsoft Azure, a leading cloud computing platform, has obtained ISO 27001 certification for its information security management system. This certification assures customers that Microsoft Azure adheres to internationally recognized standards for protecting customer data and maintaining a secure infrastructure.

4.2.4 NIST Cybersecurity Framework:

The National Institute of Standards and Technology (NIST) Cybersecurity Framework is a widely adopted framework for improving cybersecurity risk management across organizations. It provides a set of best practices, guidelines, and standards to help organizations assess and enhance their cybersecurity posture. The NIST framework consists of five core functions: Identify, Protect, Detect, Respond, and Recover. It offers flexibility, allowing organizations to adapt the framework to their unique requirements and risk profiles.

An example of NIST Cybersecurity Framework implementation is Lockheed Martin, a global aerospace and defense company. Lockheed Martin has utilized the framework to develop a comprehensive cybersecurity strategy and align its security practices with industry standards and guidelines.

4.2.5 Payment Card Industry Data Security Standard (PCI DSS):

The Payment Card Industry Data Security Standard (PCI DSS) is a set of security requirements established by major credit card companies to protect cardholder data. PCI DSS applies to organizations that store, process, or transmit cardholder data. Compliance with PCI DSS is essential for maintaining the security of payment card transactions and preventing credit card fraud. Failure to comply with PCI DSS can result in financial penalties, increased transaction fees, loss of card processing privileges, and reputational damage.

In 2013, Target Corporation, a prominent retail chain, suffered a significant data breach that compromised the payment card information of millions of customers. The breach occurred due to weaknesses in Target's network security and non-compliance with PCI DSS requirements. The incident resulted in substantial financial losses, legal actions, and damage to Target's reputation.

4.3 Staying Up-to-Date with Changing Regulations:

Cybersecurity standards and regulations are continually evolving to address emerging threats and technological advancements. To ensure compliance, non-technical executives should stay informed about changes in regulations and industry best practices. Here are some strategies to stay up-to-date:

Regularly review updates from regulatory bodies and government agencies responsible for cybersecurity, such as the National Institute of Standards and Technology (NIST), the

Information Commissioner's Office (ICO), or the Federal Trade Commission (FTC).

Engage with industry associations and professional networks that provide updates on cybersecurity regulations and standards relevant to your organization's sector.

Establish relationships with legal, compliance, and IT professionals who can provide guidance on regulatory changes and their implications for your organization.

Leverage cybersecurity consultants or third-party experts who specialize in compliance to stay informed and ensure ongoing adherence to standards and regulations.

Compliance with cybersecurity standards and regulations is an integral part of building a robust cybersecurity strategy. It helps organizations establish a baseline level of security, meet legal and regulatory requirements, and maintain trust among customers and stakeholders. By understanding the importance of compliance and staying informed about relevant standards and regulations such as GDPR, CCPA, ISO 27001, NIST Cybersecurity Framework, and PCI DSS, non-technical executives can take proactive steps to protect their organizations from cyber threats and mitigate potential risks. In the next chapter, we will explore the unique cybersecurity challenges presented by cloud-based applications and services and provide practical guidance on how to secure them effectively.

5

Chapter 5: Securing Cloud-Based Applications and Services

In today's digital landscape, cloud computing has become an integral part of business operations, offering numerous benefits such as scalability, cost-efficiency, and flexibility. However, the adoption of cloud-based applications and services also brings unique cybersecurity challenges. In this chapter, we will explore the importance of securing cloud-based applications and services, discuss the potential risks and vulnerabilities, and provide practical guidance on how non-technical executives can enhance the security of their cloud environments.

Cloud Services allow you to expand economically and with a high reliability rating

5.1 Understanding the Cloud Computing Model:

Before delving into cloud security, it is crucial to understand the cloud computing model. Cloud computing involves the delivery of on-demand computing resources, including servers, storage, databases, and software, over the internet. There are three primary service models in cloud computing:

Infrastructure as a Service (IaaS):

IaaS provides virtualized computing resources, such as virtual machines and storage, allowing organizations to build and manage their own infrastructure in the cloud.

Platform as a Service (PaaS):

PaaS offers a complete development and deployment environment in the cloud, enabling organizations to develop, test, and deploy applications without worrying about underlying infrastructure.

Software as a Service (SaaS):

SaaS delivers software applications over the internet on a subscription basis, eliminating the need for organizations to install and maintain the software on their own infrastructure.

Each service model has its own security considerations, and organizations must work with their cloud service providers to ensure the security of their applications and data.

5.2 Security Challenges in the Cloud:

5.2.1 Data Breaches and Unauthorized Access:

One of the primary concerns in the cloud environment is the risk of data breaches and unauthorized access. Cloud providers typically implement robust security measures, but organizations must also take steps to protect their data. Weak authentication mechanisms, insecure configurations, and inadequate access controls can expose sensitive data to unauthorized individuals or malicious actors.

A prominent example of a data breach in the cloud is the Capital One breach in 2019. A hacker exploited a misconfigured web application firewall (WAF) in the cloud infrastructure, gaining unauthorized access to personal information of approximately 106 million Capital One customers. The incident highlighted the importance of implementing strong access controls and regularly auditing cloud configurations to prevent unauthorized access.

5.2.2 Insecure APIs:

Application Programming Interfaces (APIs) enable communication and data exchange between cloud services and applications. However, insecure APIs can pose a significant security risk. If APIs are not properly secured, they can be vulnerable to attacks such as API abuse, injection attacks, or unauthorized API access.

For example, in 2020, a misconfigured API in the cloud-based social media management platform, SocialArks, exposed the personal information and social media account data of thousands of users. This incident underscored the need for organizations to thoroughly assess the security of APIs and implement strong authentication and authorization mechanisms.

5.2.3 Data Loss and Recovery:

Cloud providers implement robust backup and disaster recovery mechanisms, but organizations must have their own data backup and recovery strategies in place. Data loss can occur due to accidental deletion, hardware failure, or cyber attacks. Without proper backup procedures, organizations risk losing critical data and facing operational disruptions.

A recent example of data loss in the cloud occurred in 2021 when an outage at a leading cloud provider resulted in the loss of customer data for some organizations. Those without adequate backup strategies faced significant challenges in recovering their data, highlighting the importance of implementing regular backups and testing the recovery process.

5.3 Best Practices for Securing Cloud-Based Applications and Services:

5.3.1 Understand Shared Responsibility Model:

Cloud security is a shared responsibility between the cloud service provider and the organization. It is essential to understand the division of responsibilities and ensure that both parties fulfill their obligations. The cloud provider is responsible for securing the underlying infrastructure, while the organization is responsible for securing their applications, data, and user access.

5.3.2 Implement Strong Authentication and Access Controls:

Ensure that strong authentication mechanisms, such as multi-factor authentication (MFA), are in place to protect user accounts. Implement robust access controls to limit user privileges and grant access only to necessary resources. Regularly review and update user access permissions to prevent unauthorized access.

5.3.3 Encrypt Data:

Utilize encryption techniques to protect sensitive data both in transit and at rest. Encryption ensures that even if data is intercepted or stolen, it remains unintelligible to unauthorized individuals. Encrypt data before uploading it to the cloud and choose cloud services that offer encryption capabilities.

5.3.4 Regularly Monitor and Audit Cloud Environments:

Implement a robust monitoring and auditing strategy to detect and respond to security incidents promptly. Leverage cloud-native security tools and services to monitor user activity, network traffic, and application logs. Regularly review logs and conduct audits to identify any suspicious or unauthorized activities.

5.3.5 Conduct Vulnerability Assessments and Penetration Testing:

Regularly assess the security of cloud-based applications and services through vulnerability assessments and penetration testing. Identify and address any vulnerabilities or weaknesses before they can be exploited by malicious actors. Work with experienced security professionals or third-party vendors to perform thorough assessments.

5.3.6 Backup and Disaster Recovery Planning:

Implement a comprehensive backup and disaster recovery strategy for cloud-based applications and data. Regularly back up critical data and test the recovery process to ensure that data can be restored in the event of a data loss or system failure. Consider using redundant storage and geographically dispersed backup locations for enhanced resilience.

5.4 Compliance Considerations:

5.4.1 General Data Protection Regulation (GDPR):

The GDPR is a comprehensive data protection regulation that applies to organizations processing the personal data of European Union (EU) residents. When using cloud-based applications and services, organizations must ensure that the cloud provider complies with GDPR requirements. They should also review their own data processing activities to ensure compliance with GDPR principles, such as data minimization, purpose limitation, and data subject rights.

5.4.2 California Consumer Privacy Act (CCPA):

The CCPA is a state-level privacy regulation in California, USA, that grants consumers certain rights regarding their personal information. Organizations that handle the personal data of California residents must ensure compliance with CCPA when using cloud-based services. This includes understanding how personal data is collected, stored, and shared within the cloud environment and implementing necessary controls to protect consumer privacy rights.

5.4.3 International Organization for Standardization (ISO) 27001:

ISO 27001 is an internationally recognized standard for information security management systems. Organizations can use ISO 27001 as a framework to establish and maintain a robust security management system for their cloud-based applications and services. It provides a systematic approach to managing security risks and demonstrates a commitment to information security best practices.

Securing cloud-based applications and services is vital for organizations in today's digital landscape. By understanding the unique security challenges and implementing best practices, non-technical executives can enhance the security of their cloud environments. Key considerations include understanding the shared responsibility model, implementing strong authentication and access controls, encrypting data, monitoring and auditing cloud environments, conducting vulnerability assessments and penetration testing, and planning for backup and disaster recovery. Additionally, compliance with regulations such as GDPR, CCPA, and ISO 27001 ensures the protection of customer data and adherence to industry standards. In the next chapter, we will delve into the unique cybersecurity challenges presented by mobile devices and provide practical guidance on how to secure them effectively.

6

Chapter 6: Protecting Mobile Devices

Mobile devices, such as smartphones and tablets, have become an integral part of our personal and professional lives. They offer convenience, mobility, and connectivity, enabling us to stay connected, access information, and perform various tasks on the go. However, with the increasing reliance on mobile devices comes the need for robust cybersecurity measures to protect sensitive data and ensure the privacy of users. In this chapter, we will explore the unique cybersecurity challenges presented by mobile devices, provide practical guidance on how non-technical professionals can secure their mobile devices, and discuss the importance of mobile security in today's digital age.

Liberty to work on a preferred environment depends on your ability to protect your resources from malicious sources

6.1 Mobile Device Security Risks:

Mobile devices face a range of security risks that can compromise the confidentiality, integrity, and availability of data. Understanding these risks is crucial for implementing effective security measures. Let's examine some of the key risks:

6.1.1 Device Loss or Theft:

The loss or theft of a mobile device can result in unauthorized access to sensitive data. If the device is not properly protected, anyone who finds or steals it can potentially access emails, contacts, documents, and other confidential information.

6.1.2 Malicious Mobile Apps:

Malicious mobile apps are designed to deceive users or exploit vulnerabilities to gain unauthorized access to data or perform malicious activities. These apps can be disguised as legitimate applications or downloaded from unofficial app stores or malicious websites.

6.1.3 Unsecured Wi-Fi Networks:

Connecting to unsecured Wi-Fi networks, such as those in public places or coffee shops, can expose mobile devices to various security risks. Attackers can intercept network traffic, capture sensitive information, or even launch man-in-the-middle attacks.

6.1.4 Phishing Attacks:

Phishing attacks targeting mobile devices have become increasingly prevalent. Attackers send fraudulent messages or emails to trick users into revealing sensitive information, such as login credentials or financial details.

45

6.1.5 Outdated Software and Operating Systems:

Using outdated software or operating systems on mobile devices can leave them vulnerable to known security flaws. Attackers often target these vulnerabilities to gain unauthorized access or control over the device.

6.2 Best Practices for Mobile Device Security:

6.2.1 Use Strong Device Passcodes or Biometric Authentication:

Implement strong passcodes or leverage biometric authentication, such as fingerprint or facial recognition, to protect access to your mobile device. Avoid using easily guessable passcodes like "1234" or "password."

6.2.2 Keep Software and Apps Updated:

Regularly update your mobile device's operating system, firmware, and applications. Updates often include security patches that address known vulnerabilities. Enable automatic updates whenever possible to ensure that your device remains protected against the latest threats.

6.2.3 Be Cautious When Installing Apps:

Only download apps from official app stores, such as the Apple App Store or Google Play Store. Read user reviews, check app ratings, and verify the app developer's reputation before installing any new application. Be mindful of the permissions requested by apps and consider whether they are necessary for the app's functionality.

6.2.4 Enable Find My Device or Remote Wipe:

Activate the "Find My Device" feature available on most mobile devices. This feature allows you to track your device's location or remotely wipe its data in case of loss or theft. Familiarize yourself with the steps required to locate or wipe your device using this feature.

6.2.5 Use Secure Wi-Fi Networks:

Whenever possible, connect to secure Wi-Fi networks that require a password or use encryption, such as WPA2. Avoid connecting to open or public Wi-Fi networks that do not have encryption, as they are more susceptible to attacks.

6.2.6 Exercise Caution with Email and Messaging:

Be wary of unsolicited or suspicious emails, text messages, or instant messages on your mobile device. Avoid clicking on links or opening attachments from unknown or untrusted sources. When in doubt, verify the legitimacy of the message with the sender through another channel.

6.2.7 Use Mobile Security Apps:

Consider installing reputable mobile security apps that provide additional layers of protection. These apps can offer features such as malware detection, app scanning, web browsing protection, and anti-theft capabilities.

6.3 Current Examples and Real-World Scenarios:

6.3.1 Mobile Banking Trojans:

Mobile banking trojans are a type of malicious software that targets mobile banking apps and attempts to steal login credentials and other sensitive information. For example, the "BankBot" trojan targeted Android devices and disguised itself as legitimate banking apps to trick users into entering their login credentials.

6.3.2 SMS-Based Attacks:

SMS-Based attacks, also known as smishing, involve sending fraudulent SMS messages to mobile device users to trick them into revealing sensitive information or downloading malicious apps. In one case, attackers sent SMS messages impersonating a popular delivery service, prompting users to click on a malicious link that downloaded malware onto their devices.

6.3.3 Wi-Fi Eavesdropping:

Attackers can set up rogue Wi-Fi networks with names similar to legitimate networks to trick users into connecting. Once connected, they can intercept network traffic, capturing sensitive information such as usernames, passwords, or financial data. This is particularly common in public spaces like airports or coffee shops.

6.3.4 Malicious Apps:

Malicious apps disguised as popular games, utilities, or productivity tools have been found in unofficial app stores or through third-party app sources. These apps often contain malware that can compromise the security of mobile devices and the data stored on them.

6.4 Mobile Device Management (MDM):

Mobile Device Management solutions are designed to help organizations manage and secure their mobile devices. While this topic may be more relevant to IT professionals, non-technical executives should understand the benefits of implementing MDM solutions within their organizations. MDM solutions allow for centralized management of mobile devices, enabling administrators to enforce security policies, control app installations, and remotely manage and wipe devices in case of loss or theft.

Securing mobile devices is essential in today's mobile-driven world. Non-technical professionals should be aware of the risks associated with mobile devices and implement best practices to protect their devices and sensitive information. By using strong passcodes or biometric authentication, keeping software and apps updated, exercising caution with email and messaging, and using secure Wi-Fi networks, individuals can significantly enhance the security of their mobile devices. Additionally, being mindful of current examples and real-world scenarios helps to understand the evolving threat landscape. In the next chapter, we will explore the unique cybersecurity challenges presented by Internet of Things (IoT) devices and provide practical guidance on how to secure them effectively.

7

Chapter 7: Securing the Internet of Things (IoT)

The Internet of Things (IoT) has revolutionized the way we interact with technology and the world around us. IoT devices, such as smart home devices, wearable, and industrial sensors, are interconnected and capable of collecting and exchanging data. While IoT offers numerous benefits and conveniences, it also presents unique cybersecurity challenges. In this chapter, we will explore the importance of securing IoT devices, discuss the risks associated with IoT, and provide practical guidance on how non-technical professionals can protect their IoT devices and data.

IoT opens a myriad of possibilities... and threats

7.1 Understanding the Risks of IoT:

IoT devices are vulnerable to a range of security risks that can have severe consequences if not addressed. Let's examine some of the key risks associated with IoT:

7.1.1 Weak Authentication and Authorization:

Many IoT devices come with default or weak authentication mechanisms, making them easy targets for unauthorized access. Attackers can exploit these vulnerabilities to gain control over the devices or gain access to the data they collect.

7.1.2 Lack of Encryption:

Inadequate or absent encryption protocols in IoT devices can expose sensitive data to interception or tampering. Without encryption, the data transmitted between IoT devices and their associated systems can be easily accessed by malicious actors.

7.1.3 Vulnerabilities in Firmware and Software:

IoT devices often rely on firmware and software to function. However, these components may contain vulnerabilities that can be exploited by attackers. Without regular updates and patches, IoT devices remain susceptible to known security flaws.

7.1.4 Insecure Communication Protocols:

IoT devices communicate with each other and with other systems through various protocols. Insecure or outdated communication protocols can be targeted by attackers to intercept or manipulate the data transmitted by IoT devices.

7.1.5 Lack of Physical Security:

Physical security is often overlooked in the context of IoT devices. Unauthorized physical access to IoT devices can result in tampering, data theft, or the introduction of malicious components.

7.2 Best Practices for Securing IoT Devices:

7.2.1 Change Default Credentials:

One of the first steps to secure IoT devices is to change the default usernames and passwords. Use strong, unique passwords for each device and ensure that they are not easily guessable.

7.2.2 Keep Firmware and Software Updated:

Regularly update the firmware and software of IoT devices. Manufacturers often release patches and updates to address security vulnerabilities. Check for updates periodically or enable automatic updates if available.

7.2.3 Implement Network Segmentation:

Segmenting your network isolates IoT devices from critical systems and sensitive data. By creating separate network segments, you limit the potential impact of a compromised IoT device.

7.2.4 Use Secure Communication Protocols:

Ensure that IoT devices communicate over secure protocols, such as HTTPS or TLS, to encrypt data in transit. Avoid using insecure protocols like HTTP or FTP.

7.2.5 Disable Unused Features and Services.

Disable any features or services on IoT devices that are not essential for their intended use. Unused features can introduce additional vulnerabilities that can be exploited by attackers.

7.2.6 Conduct Vulnerability Assessments:

Regularly assess the security of your IoT devices by conducting vulnerability assessments or engaging third-party security professionals. Identify any potential weaknesses or vulnerabilities and take appropriate remediation actions.

7.2.7 Establish a Secure Password Management Process:

Develop a secure password management process for IoT devices. This includes using password managers, enforcing password complexity requirements, and regularly updating passwords.

7.3 Current Examples and Real-World Scenarios:

7.3.1 Mirai Botnet:

The Mirai botnet is a prominent example of how insecure IoT devices can be harnessed for malicious purposes. In 2016, the Mirai botnet was responsible for launching massive distributed denial-of-service (DDoS) attacks by exploiting vulnerabilities in IoT devices with weak security. This incident highlights the importance of securing IoT devices to prevent them from being weaponized by attackers.

7.3.2 Smart Home Vulnerabilities:

Smart home devices, such as smart locks, security cameras, and thermostats, have been found to have vulnerabilities that expose users to potential risks. For instance, some smart locks have been susceptible to hacking, allowing unauthorized access to homes. It underscores the need for robust security measures to protect IoT devices within our homes.

7.3.3 Industrial IoT Security Incidents:

In industrial settings, IoT devices are often used to monitor and control critical infrastructure. However, several security incidents have highlighted the risks associated with insecure industrial IoT devices. For example, a 2017 cyber attack targeted a petrochemical plant in Saudi Arabia, causing significant disruptions. This incident underscores the importance of securing IoT devices in industrial environments to safeguard critical infrastructure.

Securing IoT devices is crucial to protect sensitive data, main-

tain privacy, and mitigate the risks associated with interconnected systems. By understanding the unique risks posed by
IoT, implementing best practices such as changing default credentials, keeping firmware and software updated, segmenting
networks, using secure communication protocols, disabling
unused features, conducting vulnerability assessments, and
establishing a secure password management process, non-
technical professionals can significantly enhance the security
posture of their IoT devices. In the next chapter, we will explore
the concept of cybersecurity insurance and its importance for
businesses in mitigating financial risks associated with cyber
incidents.

8

Chapter 8: Cybersecurity Insurance

As the threat landscape continues to evolve, organizations face increasing risks of cyber attacks and data breaches. The financial implications of such incidents can be significant, including costs associated with remediation, legal expenses, regulatory fines, and reputational damage. Cybersecurity insurance, also known as cyber insurance or cyber liability insurance, is an emerging solution that helps businesses mitigate the financial risks associated with cyber incidents. In this chapter, we will explore what cybersecurity insurance is, what it covers, and how non-technical professionals can make informed decisions when selecting a policy for their organization.

Insurance not only protects you, it gives you a clear image of your security needs

8.1 Understanding Cybersecurity Insurance:

Cybersecurity insurance is a type of insurance coverage designed to protect organizations from financial losses resulting from cyber incidents. It is specifically tailored to address the unique risks and challenges posed by cyber threats. Cyber insurance policies typically provide coverage for various aspects of a cyber incident, including data breaches, network security failures, and business interruption.

8.1.1 Coverage for Data Breaches:

Data breaches involve unauthorized access or disclosure of sensitive data, such as customer information, employee records, or intellectual property. Cyber insurance policies typically cover the costs associated with investigating and responding to data breaches, including forensic investigations, notifying affected individuals, providing credit monitoring services, and legal expenses.

8.1.2 Coverage for Business Interruption:

Cyber incidents can disrupt business operations, leading to financial losses. Cyber insurance policies may cover expenses related to business interruption, such as loss of revenue, additional expenses incurred to restore systems and operations, and reputational damage mitigation efforts.

8.1.3 Coverage for Extortion and Ransomware:

Ransomware attacks, where cybercriminals encrypt data and demand a ransom for its release, have become increasingly common. Cyber insurance policies may cover the costs associated with ransom payments, negotiations with attackers, and restoring systems following an attack.

8.1.4 Coverage for Privacy Liability:

Privacy liability refers to the legal obligations organizations have to protect the personal information of individuals. Cyber insurance policies often provide coverage for legal expenses and damages resulting from privacy breaches, including lawsuits and regulatory fines.

8.2 Assessing Cybersecurity Insurance Needs:

8.2.1 Evaluate Existing Cybersecurity Measures:

Before purchasing a cyber insurance policy, it is essential to assess your organization's current cybersecurity posture. Identify the security measures and protocols already in place, including firewalls, antivirus software, employee training programs, and incident response plans. This evaluation helps determine any gaps in coverage and informs the selection of an appropriate insurance policy.

8.2.2 Conduct a Risk Assessment:

Understand the specific risks your organization faces. Consider factors such as the sensitivity of the data you handle, the industry you operate in, the size of your organization, and the regulatory environment. A comprehensive risk assessment can guide you in selecting the appropriate coverage limits and policy options.

8.2.3 Review Regulatory Requirements:

Depending on your industry and geographical location, there may be legal or regulatory requirements for cybersecurity insurance. Familiarize yourself with relevant laws and regulations to ensure compliance and to understand any specific coverage requirements.

8.3 Selecting a Cybersecurity Insurance Policy:

8.3.1 Coverage Types and Limits:

Carefully review the coverage types offered by different insurance providers and ensure they align with your organization's specific needs. Consider the policy's coverage limits, sub-limits, and deductibles. Assess whether the policy adequately covers the potential financial impact of a cyber incident, including the costs of investigation, notification, legal defense, and business interruption.

8.3.2 Exclusions and Conditions:

Pay attention to any exclusions or conditions outlined in the policy. Exclusions may limit coverage for specific types of incidents or circumstances. Conditions may include requirements for implementing specific security measures or adhering to specific incident response protocols. Ensure that you understand and can comply with the policy's conditions.

8.3.3 Retroactive Date and Prior Acts Coverage:

Some policies may have a retroactive date that specifies the period for which coverage is provided for prior acts. Understand the retroactive date and ensure it aligns with your organization's specific needs. If your organization had prior cybersecurity incidents, ensure that such incidents are covered by the policy.

8.3.4 Subrogation and Aggregation Clauses:

Subrogation clauses determine whether the insurance provider can pursue legal action against a third party responsible for a cyber incident. Aggregation clauses govern how the insurance provider calculates losses when multiple cyber incidents occur within a specific period. Review these clauses to understand their implications for your organization.

8.4 Cybersecurity Insurance and Risk Mitigation:

8.4.1 Risk Management and Loss Control:

Cybersecurity insurance is not a substitute for effective risk management practices. Implement robust cybersecurity measures, including regular vulnerability assessments, employee training, incident response planning, and secure data management. Insurers may offer discounts or favorable terms for organizations that demonstrate proactive risk mitigation efforts.

8.4.2 Incident Response Preparedness:

An incident response plan is crucial for effective management of cyber incidents. Review your organization's incident response procedures and ensure they align with the requirements outlined by the insurance policy. Regularly update and test your incident response plan to address emerging threats and ensure its effectiveness.

8.5 Staying Informed and Engaging with Insurers:

8.5.1 Monitoring the Cyber Insurance Market:

The cybersecurity insurance landscape is continually evolving. Stay informed about the latest trends, policy options, and changes in the market. Regularly assess your organization's insurance needs and consider reevaluating your policy as circumstances change.

8.5.2 Engaging with Insurers and Brokers:

Establish a relationship with your insurance provider or broker. Engage in discussions to gain a deeper understanding of policy terms and coverage options. Seek their expertise to ensure you have the right coverage and to address any concerns or questions.

8.6 Real-World Examples:

8.6.1 Equifax Data Breach:

In 2017, Equifax, one of the largest credit reporting agencies, experienced a massive data breach that exposed sensitive information of approximately 147 million individuals. The incident resulted in significant financial losses, reputational damage, legal expenses, and regulatory fines. Equifax had cybersecurity insurance in place, which helped mitigate some of the financial impact.

8.6.2 NotPetya Ransomware Attack:

The 2017 NotPetya ransomware attack targeted organizations worldwide, causing widespread disruption and financial losses. Several affected organizations relied on cyber insurance to cover the costs associated with remediation, business interruption, and reputational damage.

8.6.3 GDPR and Regulatory Fines:

With the introduction of the General Data Protection Regulation (GDPR) in the European Union, organizations face the risk of substantial fines for non-compliance with data protection requirements. Cybersecurity insurance can help cover the costs of fines and legal expenses resulting from regulatory enforcement actions.

In conclusion, cybersecurity insurance plays a vital role in mitigating the financial risks associated with cyber incidents.

By understanding the coverage types, conducting thorough assessments, selecting the right policy, implementing effective risk mitigation measures, and engaging with insurers, non-technical professionals can make informed decisions to protect their organizations from the financial impact of cyber threats. In the next chapter, we will explore the importance of recruiting cybersecurity talent and building a skilled workforce to enhance an organization's security posture.

9

Chapter 9: Recruiting Cybersecurity Talent

In today's digital landscape, the demand for skilled cyberse-curity professionals continues to outpace the available supply. Organizations across industries are facing an increasing need for qualified individuals who can protect their valuable assets from cyber threats. In this chapter, we will delve into the impor-tance of recruiting cybersecurity talent and provide guidance for non-technical professionals on how to identify the skills and experience needed for different cybersecurity roles. We will also explore the differences between technical leaders and cybersecurity managers, as well as provide real-world examples to illustrate the importance of hiring the right cybersecurity talent.

Recruiting from within the company raises loyalty and reduces the learning curve

9.1 The Importance of Cybersecurity Talent:
9.1.1 Growing Cyber Threat Landscape:

As cyber threats become more sophisticated and prevalent, organizations must bolster their cybersecurity capabilities. Skilled cybersecurity professionals play a critical role in detecting and mitigating these threats, ensuring the confiden-tiality, integrity, and availability of sensitive data and systems.

9.1.2 Impact of Cybersecurity Incidents:

Cybersecurity incidents can have significant financial, legal, and reputational consequences. A strong cybersecurity team with the right expertise can help prevent and respond effectively to incidents, minimizing the impact on the organization.

9.1.3 Compliance and Regulatory Requirements:

Many industries have specific cybersecurity compliance and regulatory requirements that organizations must meet. Hiring cybersecurity professionals who understand these requirements and can implement appropriate controls is essential for maintaining compliance and avoiding penalties.

9.2 Identifying the Skills and Experience Needed:

9.2.1 Technical Skills:

Different cybersecurity roles require specific technical skills. For example, a network security engineer should have expertise in network protocols, firewalls, intrusion detection systems, and vulnerability assessment tools. A threat intelligence analyst needs knowledge of threat intelligence platforms, malware analysis, and incident response techniques. Identify the technical skills required for each role to ensure that candidates possess the necessary expertise.

9.2.2 Knowledge of Security Frameworks and Standards:

Familiarity with industry-recognized security frameworks and standards, such as ISO 27001, NIST Cybersecurity Framework, or CIS Controls, is essential. These frameworks provide a road map for implementing effective security controls. Look for candidates who have experience aligning security practices with these frameworks.

9.2.3 Soft Skills:

Cybersecurity professionals must possess excellent communication, problem-solving, and analytical skills. They should be able to effectively communicate complex security concepts to both technical and non-technical stakeholders. Look for candidates who can work collaboratively, adapt to evolving threats, and think critically in high-pressure situations.

9.2.4 Continuous Learning and Adaptability:

The cybersecurity landscape is constantly evolving. Look for candidates who demonstrate a commitment to continuous learning and staying updated on emerging threats, industry trends, and new technologies. Seek individuals who are adaptable and can quickly learn new tools and techniques.

9.3 Technical Leaders vs. Cybersecurity Managers:

9.3.1 Technical Leaders:

Technical leaders in cybersecurity are responsible for the hands-on implementation and management of security controls. They have deep technical expertise and often hold specialized certifications such as Certified Information Systems Security Professional (CISSP) or Certified Ethical Hacker (CEH). Technical leaders play a crucial role in designing and implementing effective security measures, conducting vulnerability assessments, and responding to incidents.

9.3.2 Cybersecurity Managers:

Cybersecurity managers oversee the strategic planning, policy development, and coordination of cybersecurity initiatives within an organization. While they may have a technical background, their primary focus is on managing the cybersecurity program, ensuring compliance with regulations, and aligning security objectives with business goals. Cybersecurity managers often hold certifications such as Certified Information Security

Manager (CISM) or Certified Information Systems Auditor (CISA).

9.4 Real-World Examples:

9.4.1 SolarWinds Supply Chain Attack:

The SolarWinds supply chain attack, discovered in 2020, exposed vulnerabilities in software supply chains, affecting numerous organizations and government agencies. Hiring cybersecurity professionals with expertise in supply chain security and the ability to assess and mitigate such risks could have helped organizations identify and respond to the attack more effectively.

9.4.2 Ransomware Attacks on Healthcare Organizations:

Healthcare organizations have been frequent targets of ransomware attacks, resulting in disrupted services, compromised patient data, and financial losses. Hiring cybersecurity professionals with experience in healthcare security and knowledge of specific industry regulations, such as the Health Insurance Portability and Accountability Act (HIPAA), is crucial for protecting patient privacy and maintaining the integrity of critical healthcare systems.

9.4.3 Talent Shortage in the Cybersecurity Industry:

The global shortage of skilled cybersecurity professionals poses a significant challenge for organizations. The 2021 Cybersecurity Workforce Study by (ISC)² estimated a shortage of 3.12 million cybersecurity professionals worldwide. This shortage emphasizes the importance of robust recruitment strategies, talent development programs, and creative approaches to attract and retain cybersecurity talent.

9.5 Recruitment Strategies:

9.5.1 Networking and Industry Engagement:

Develop relationships with industry professionals, attend cybersecurity conferences and events, and engage with cybersecurity communities to expand your network. Networking can help you identify potential candidates and gain insights into emerging trends and best practices.

9.5.2 Collaborating with Academic Institutions:

Partnering with academic institutions that offer cybersecurity programs can be an effective way to recruit talent. Establish relationships with professors and students, offer internships or apprenticeships, and participate in career fairs to attract young talent with a passion for cybersecurity.

9.5.3 Leveraging Professional Associations and Certifications:

Engage with professional associations and certification bodies such as (ISC)^2, CompTIA, or ISACA. These organizations provide resources for job postings, professional development, and access to a network of certified professionals.

9.5.4 Non-Traditional Talent Sources:

Consider candidates with non-traditional backgrounds, such as individuals transitioning from the military, law enforcement, or other technical fields. Many skills acquired in these fields, such as critical thinking, problem-solving, and attention to detail, can be transferable to cybersecurity roles.

9.6 Developing a Skilled Workforce:

9.6.1 Training and Professional Development:

Invest in training and professional development opportunities for your cybersecurity team. Encourage them to pursue industry certifications and attend relevant workshops and conferences. Continuous learning not only enhances their skills but also demonstrates your commitment to their growth and development.

9.6.2 Mentorship Programs:

Implement mentorship programs within your organization to foster knowledge transfer and skill development. Pair experienced cybersecurity professionals with junior team members to provide guidance, support, and career advice.

9.6.3 Retention Strategies:

Retaining cybersecurity talent is as crucial as recruiting it. Develop a positive work environment, offer competitive compensation and benefits, and provide opportunities for career advancement. Recognize and reward exceptional performance to foster loyalty and retention.

In conclusion, recruiting and retaining skilled cybersecurity professionals is vital for organizations to effectively combat the ever-evolving landscape of cyber threats. By understanding the necessary skills, differentiating between technical leaders and cybersecurity managers, and implementing effective recruitment strategies, non-technical professionals can contribute to building a robust cybersecurity workforce. In the next chapter, we will explore the importance of managing third-party cybersecurity risks and best practices for vendor management.

10

Chapter 10: Managing Third-Party Cybersecurity Risks

In today's interconnected business landscape, organizations often rely on third-party vendors and partners to deliver products, services, and critical infrastructure components. However, this dependence on external entities introduces new cybersecurity risks. In this chapter, we will explore the cybersecurity risks associated with working with third-party vendors and provide practical guidance on how to assess and manage these risks. We will discuss best practices for vendor management, due diligence, and contractual agreements. Through real-world examples, we will highlight the importance of managing third-party cybersecurity risks and the potential consequences of failing to do so.

Delegating the services our company needs on another, requires constant communication, strategy and metrics.

10.1 Understanding Third-Party Cybersecurity Risks:
10.1.1 Expanded Attack Surface:

When organizations engage with third-party vendors, they effectively expand their attack surface. An attack on a vendor's systems or infrastructure can have a ripple effect, compromising the security of the organization's networks, data, and operations.

10.1.2 Shared Data and Access:

Third-party vendors often have access to sensitive data, systems, or networks. If their security controls are insufficient, it could lead to unauthorized access, data breaches, or even sabotage. It is essential to assess the security posture of vendors and ensure that appropriate measures are in place to protect shared data and assets.

10.1.3 Regulatory Compliance:

Organizations may be subject to industry-specific regulations and standards that require them to ensure the security and privacy of customer data even when it is shared with third parties. Failure to manage third-party cybersecurity risks can result in non-compliance and potential legal and financial consequences.

10.2 Best Practices for Managing Third-Party Cybersecurity Risks:

10.2.1 Vendor Risk Assessment:

Conducting a comprehensive vendor risk assessment is a crucial step in managing third-party cybersecurity risks. Assess the vendors' security controls, practices, and track record to evaluate their ability to protect your organization's data and systems. Consider factors such as their security policies, incident response capabilities, and their compliance with relevant security standards.

10.2.2 Due Diligence:

Before engaging with a third-party vendor, perform due diligence to gather information about their reputation, financial stability, and security practices. Request references and conduct background checks to ensure that you are working with a reputable and trustworthy partner.

10.2.3 Security Requirements in Contracts:

Include specific cybersecurity requirements in contracts with third-party vendors. Clearly define expectations regarding security controls, incident response procedures, data protection measures, and compliance with applicable regulations. Contractual agreements should also address the consequences of non-compliance and establish mechanisms for regular security audits and assessments.

10.2.4 Ongoing Monitoring and Auditing:

Vendor management should not end with the signing of a contract. Establish a process for ongoing monitoring and auditing of vendors' security practices. Regularly assess their security controls, review audit reports, and conduct penetration tests or vulnerability assessments to ensure that security standards are upheld throughout the partnership.

10.2.5 Incident Response and Notification:

Define the roles, responsibilities, and communication protocols for handling cybersecurity incidents involving third-party vendors. Establish clear procedures for incident response, including the timely notification of any security breaches or incidents. Collaborate with vendors to develop joint incident response plans and ensure alignment in addressing potential threats.

10.3 Real-World Examples:

10.3.1 Target Data Breach:

The Target data breach in 2013 serves as a prominent example of the risks associated with third-party vendors. Attackers gained access to Target's network by compromising a third-party HVAC vendor, which had access to Target's systems. This breach resulted in the theft of personal and financial data of millions of customers and had severe financial and reputational implications for Target.

10.3.2 Supply Chain Attacks:

The SolarWinds supply chain attack in 2020 highlighted the potential impact of compromised software vendors on organizations' security. Hackers infiltrated SolarWinds' software development process, leading to the distribution of a malicious update to thousands of organizations worldwide. This incident demonstrated the need for robust supply chain security practices and thorough vetting of software vendors.

10.3.3 Cloud Service Providers:

Organizations often rely on cloud service providers (CSPs) to store and process their data. While CSPs generally offer robust security measures, organizations must still assess their security capabilities and contractual obligations. In 2021, a misconfigured AWS S3 bucket exposed sensitive data from multiple organizations, highlighting the importance of understanding shared responsibility models and conducting proper due diligence when selecting and managing CSPs.

Effectively managing third-party cybersecurity risks is vital for safeguarding organizational assets, data, and reputation. By conducting comprehensive risk assessments, practicing due diligence, incorporating security requirements into contracts, and maintaining ongoing monitoring and auditing, organizations can mitigate the potential risks associated with third-party vendors. In the next chapter, we will explore the steps organizations need to take in responding to cybersecurity incidents, including incident detection, containment, and recovery.

11

Chapter 11: Responding to Cybersecurity Incidents

In today's digital landscape, no organization is immune to cyber threats. Despite implementing robust security measures, the possibility of a cybersecurity incident remains. In this chapter, we will explore the steps that organizations need to take in responding to cybersecurity incidents. We will discuss incident detection, containment, and recovery strategies, and provide practical guidance for effective incident response. Through real-world examples, we will emphasize the importance of having an incident response plan and highlight the potential consequences of mishandling cybersecurity incidents.

Identifying, Responding and Mitigating incidents can make all the difference for the correct functioning of the company

11.1 Incident Detection:
11.1.1 Monitoring and Alert Systems:

Implementing robust monitoring systems, such as intrusion detection systems (IDS) and security information and event management (SIEM) tools, is crucial for timely incident detection. These systems analyze network traffic, log files, and other relevant data sources to identify suspicious activities or indicators of compromise.

11.1.2 Threat Intelligence:

Leverage threat intelligence sources to stay informed about the latest threats and attack techniques. Subscribing to threat intelligence feeds, collaborating with industry groups, and monitoring open-source intelligence can provide valuable insights to help detect and respond to emerging threats.

11.1.3 User Awareness and Reporting:

Educate employees about the signs of a potential cybersecurity incident and encourage them to report any suspicious activities promptly. Establish clear channels for reporting incidents, such as a dedicated email address or an incident response hotline.

11.2 Incident Containment:
11.2.1 Isolation and Segmentation:

When an incident is detected, isolate affected systems or networks to prevent the spread of the attack. Segmentation helps contain the impact by limiting access between different parts of the network, thereby reducing the attacker's ability to move laterally.

11.2.2 Disconnecting Compromised Systems:

In some cases, it may be necessary to disconnect compromised systems from the network to prevent further damage. However, careful consideration should be given to the potential impact on business operations and the need for forensic analysis.

11.2.3 Incident Triage:

Conduct an initial assessment of the incident to determine its scope, impact, and severity. Prioritize actions based on the criticality of affected systems and data, focusing on containment measures that can limit the attacker's access and mitigate further harm.

11.3 Incident Recovery:

11.3.1 Incident Response Team Activation:

Activate the incident response team promptly after the incident is detected. The team should include representatives from various departments, including IT, legal, communications, and senior management. Assign specific roles and responsibilities to team members to ensure an organized and coordinated response.

11.3.2 Forensic Investigation:

Engage a qualified forensics team to conduct a thorough investigation into the incident. Forensic analysis aims to determine the cause of the incident, identify compromised systems or data, collect evidence for potential legal proceedings, and gather insights to strengthen future defenses.

11.3.3 System Restoration:

Once the incident has been contained and analyzed, proceed with system restoration. This involves rebuilding affected systems, applying patches or updates to address vulnerabilities, and ensuring that systems are secure before reconnecting them to the network.

11.3.4 Communication and Notification:

Develop a communication plan to inform internal stakeholders, customers, partners, and relevant authorities about the incident. Timely and transparent communication helps maintain trust, manage reputation, and meet regulatory requirements.

11.4 Real-World Examples:

11.4.1 Equifax Data Breach:

The Equifax data breach in 2017 serves as a significant example of the importance of effective incident response. Attackers exploited a vulnerability in Equifax's systems, resulting in the exposure of sensitive personal and financial data of approximately 147 million individuals. The incident not only led to substantial financial losses but also severely damaged Equifax's reputation and triggered legal repercussions.

11.4.2 Colonial Pipeline Ransomware Attack:

In May 2021, the Colonial Pipeline, which supplies fuel to a significant portion of the United States, fell victim to a ransomware attack. The attack disrupted fuel supplies and led to panic buying in several states. The incident highlighted the criticality of incident response in the face of ransomware attacks and the potential impact on critical infrastructure.

11.4.3 NotPetya Global Malware Outbreak:

The NotPetya malware outbreak in 2017 affected numerous organizations worldwide, including major shipping company Maersk, causing significant disruptions to their operations. The incident underscored the importance of effective incident response, including timely communication, cooperation with law enforcement, and the implementation of robust backup and recovery processes.

Proper incident response is crucial for minimizing the impact of cybersecurity incidents and facilitating recovery. By establishing incident detection capabilities, implementing effective containment strategies, and following a well-defined incident response plan, organizations can effectively mitigate the potential damage caused by cyber attacks. In the next chapter, we will explore the unique cybersecurity challenges presented by remote work and provide practical guidance on securing remote work environments.

12

Chapter 12: Cybersecurity for Remote Work

The rise of remote work has revolutionized the modern work-place, providing flexibility and convenience. However, it has also introduced unique cybersecurity challenges. In this chapter, we will explore the security risks associated with remote work and provide practical guidance on how to secure remote work environments. Through real-world examples, we will highlight the importance of implementing effective security measures to protect both employees and organizations in the remote work era.

The ability to work anywhere raises the competitiveness of any business

12.1 The Unique Challenges of Remote Work:

12.1.1 Use of Personal Devices:

Remote work often involves employees using their personal devices for work-related tasks. While this brings convenience, it also raises security concerns. Personal devices may lack the necessary security controls and may be more susceptible to malware infections or unauthorized access.

12.1.2 Unsecured Networks:

Working remotely means connecting to various networks, including home Wi-Fi networks, public Wi-Fi hotspots, or shared networks. These networks can be vulnerable to eavesdropping and man-in-the-middle attacks, potentially exposing sensitive data.

12.1.3 Phishing and Social Engineering:

Attackers often exploit the distractions and uncertainties associated with remote work to launch phishing attacks or engage in social engineering tactics. Employees may be more susceptible to falling for these scams, potentially compromising sensitive information or providing access to corporate systems.

12.2 Securing Remote Work Environments:

12.2.1 Secure Network Connections:

Encourage the use of virtual private networks (VPNs) to establish secure connections between remote employees and corporate networks. VPNs encrypt data transmitted over the network, protecting it from unauthorized access.

12.2.2 Multi-Factor Authentication:

Implement multi-factor authentication (MFA) for remote access to corporate resources. MFA adds an extra layer of security by requiring users to provide multiple forms of identification, such as a password and a unique code generated by a mobile app or sent via SMS.

12.2.3 Endpoint Security:

Ensure that remote devices have adequate endpoint security measures in place, such as up-to-date antivirus software, firewalls, and regular patching. Encourage employees to use company-provided devices whenever possible, as they can be better managed and secured.

12.2.4 Employee Education and Awareness:

Train remote employees on cybersecurity best practices, including identifying and avoiding phishing emails, using strong and unique passwords, and recognizing suspicious activities. Regularly communicate security updates and reminders to reinforce good security habits.

12.2.5 Data Protection and Encryption:

Implement data protection measures, such as data encryption and data loss prevention (DLP) solutions, to safeguard sensitive information. Encryption ensures that data remains protected even if it is intercepted or accessed by unauthorized parties.

12.2.6 Secure Collaboration Tools:

Select and use secure collaboration tools that provide end-to-end encryption and strong access controls. Ensure that employees are trained on the proper use of these tools and understand the importance of protecting confidential information.

12.3 Real-World Examples:

12.3.1 Zoom Security and Privacy Concerns:

During the COVID-19 pandemic, the widespread adoption of video conferencing tools, such as Zoom, highlighted the importance of securing remote collaboration platforms. Zoom faced scrutiny for security and privacy issues, including unauthorized access to meetings (so-called "Zoom bombings") and data privacy concerns. These incidents emphasized the need for organizations to carefully evaluate and configure collaboration tools to maintain a secure remote work environment.

12.3.2 Remote Desktop Protocol (RDP) Attacks:

Remote Desktop Protocol (RDP) is a commonly used remote access tool. However, misconfigured RDP services have been exploited by attackers to gain unauthorized access to corporate networks. The increase in remote work has amplified the risks associated with RDP attacks, reinforcing the need for strong authentication, secure configurations, and monitoring of remote access services.

12.4 Managing Remote Work Policies:

12.4.1 Acceptable Use Policies:

Establish clear remote work policies that outline acceptable use of personal devices, network connections, and collaboration tools. These policies should also address data protection, employee responsibilities, and consequences for non-compliance.

12.4.2 Regular Assessments and Audits:

Conduct regular assessments and audits to identify vulnerabilities, evaluate the effectiveness of security controls, and ensure compliance with remote work security policies. This includes evaluating the security posture of employee devices, network configurations, and remote access mechanisms.

12.4.3 Incident Response for Remote Incidents:

Develop an incident response plan specific to remote incidents, including procedures for reporting and investigating security incidents. Remote work introduces unique challenges for incident response, and organizations need to be prepared to respond promptly and effectively to mitigate potential damage.

As remote work becomes increasingly prevalent, organizations must adapt their cybersecurity strategies to address the unique challenges it presents. Securing remote work environments requires a combination of technical controls, employee education, and robust policies. By implementing the recommended security measures and staying vigilant, organizations can protect their sensitive data and maintain a secure remote work environment. In the next chapter, we will explore the future trends in cybersecurity and discuss emerging threats and technologies that organizations should be aware of.

13

Chapter 13: Future Trends in Cybersecurity

The field of cybersecurity is dynamic and constantly evolving. In this chapter, we will explore future trends in cybersecurity, including emerging threats and technologies. Understanding these trends is crucial for organizations to stay ahead of cyber threats and proactively adapt their security strategies. We will discuss the potential impact of technologies such as artificial intelligence (AI), quantum computing, and the Internet of Things (IoT) on cybersecurity. Through real-world examples, we will illustrate the importance of staying informed about future trends to protect against evolving threats.

Vision of the future is one of the best ways to perform business

13.1 Artificial Intelligence and Machine Learning in Cybersecurity:

13.1.1 AI-Driven Cyber Attacks:

As artificial intelligence advances, cybercriminals are increasingly leveraging AI to automate and enhance their attacks. AI-driven malware, chatbots, and social engineering techniques can make attacks more sophisticated and difficult to detect. For example, AI-powered chatbots can convincingly mimic human behavior to deceive users and extract sensitive information.

13.1.2 AI-Powered Cybersecurity Defenses:

On the defensive side, AI and machine learning are being utilized to develop advanced cybersecurity solutions. AI algorithms can analyze vast amounts of data, identify patterns, and detect anomalies to identify potential threats. Machine learning models can continuously learn and adapt to new attack vectors, improving the effectiveness of security measures.

13.2 Quantum Computing and its Implications for Cybersecurity:

13.2.1 Quantum Computing Threats:

Quantum computing has the potential to break commonly used cryptographic algorithms, posing a significant threat to existing encryption methods. Quantum computers can perform complex calculations much faster than classical computers, potentially rendering current encryption algorithms obsolete. This could compromise the confidentiality and integrity of sensitive data.

13.2.2 Post-Quantum Cryptography:

To address the quantum computing threat, researchers are developing post-quantum cryptography (PQC) algorithms that can withstand quantum attacks. PQC aims to provide encryption methods that are resistant to attacks from both classical and quantum computers. Organizations will need to prepare for the transition to post-quantum cryptographic algorithms to ensure the security of their data in the quantum era.

13.3 Internet of Things (IoT) Security Challenges:

13.3.1 Vulnerabilities in IoT Devices:

The proliferation of IoT devices introduces new security risks. Many IoT devices have limited computing power and lack robust security features, making them vulnerable to exploitation. Compromised IoT devices can be used as entry points into networks or launch pads for distributed denial-of-service (DDoS) attacks.

13.3.2 Botnets and IoT-Based Attacks:

The Mirai botnet attack in 2016 demonstrated the potential of IoT-based attacks. Mirai exploited poorly secured IoT devices, turning them into a massive botnet that targeted critical internet infrastructure. This attack highlighted the urgent need for improved security standards and practices for IoT devices.

13.4 Cloud Security and the Shift to Cloud-Native Environments:

13.4.1 Cloud Security Concerns:

As organizations increasingly adopt cloud computing, security concerns have emerged. Misconfigured cloud environments, insecure APIs, and data breaches in cloud storage systems have raised alarms. Cloud providers and organizations must work together to ensure robust security measures are in place.

13.4.2 DevSecOps and Cloud-Native Security:

The shift towards cloud-native architectures requires organizations to adopt a DevSecOps approach, integrating security practices into the entire software development and deployment lifecycle. DevSecOps emphasizes automating security processes, incorporating security controls into code, and continuously monitoring and assessing cloud-native environments.

13.5 Emerging Threats: Deepfakes and Synthetic Identity Theft:

13.5.1 Deepfake Technology:

Deepfakes are synthetic media, often videos, created using artificial intelligence techniques. They can manipulate or fabricate content to make it appear authentic. Deepfakes pose significant risks for individuals and organizations, as they can be used for disinformation campaigns, impersonation, or blackmail.

13.5.2 Synthetic Identity Theft:

Synthetic identity theft involves creating fictional identities by combining real and fabricated personal information. This technique makes it difficult for traditional identity verification methods to detect fraudulent activities. Criminals can exploit synthetic identities for financial fraud, opening accounts, and evading law enforcement.

13.6 Cybersecurity Workforce Challenges:

13.6.1 Shortage of Skilled Professionals:
  The demand for cybersecurity professionals exceeds the available talent pool. Organizations struggle to find skilled personnel who can understand evolving threats, implement effective security measures, and respond to incidents. Addressing the cybersecurity skills gap is crucial for organizations to protect against emerging threats.

13.6.2 Automation and Artificial Intelligence:

Automation and AI can help alleviate the shortage of skilled professionals by augmenting existing cybersecurity teams. AI can assist in threat intelligence, incident response, and security monitoring. Automation can streamline routine tasks, allowing professionals to focus on more complex challenges.

As the digital landscape evolves, so do cyber threats. Organizations must stay informed about future trends in cybersecurity to adapt their strategies and protect their critical assets. The advancements in artificial intelligence, quantum computing, IoT, and other emerging technologies present both opportunities and challenges. By understanding these trends and proactively addressing them, organizations can mitigate risks and maintain a resilient cybersecurity posture. In the final chapter, we will summarize the key insights from the book and emphasize the importance of a comprehensive cybersecurity approach.

14

Conclusion

In this final chapter, we will summarize the key insights and takeaways from the book "Cybersecurity for Non-Technical Executives." Throughout the preceding chapters, we explored the importance of cybersecurity for businesses and provided guidance on various aspects of cybersecurity strategy and implementation. In this chapter, we will reiterate the key points and emphasize the crucial role that non-technical executives play in ensuring the security and resilience of their organizations.

The Business Impact of Ignoring Cybersecurity:

Throughout the book, we highlighted the potential consequences of ignoring cybersecurity. From financial losses and reputational damage to legal liability and regulatory non-compliance, the impact of a cybersecurity breach can be severe. The examples we discussed, such as the Equifax data breach and the NotPetya ransomware attack, demonstrate the far-reaching consequences that organizations face when cybersecurity is not prioritized.

The Evolving Threat Landscape:

We explored various types of cybersecurity threats, ranging from malware and phishing attacks to supply chain compromises and IoT vulnerabilities. The threat landscape is constantly evolving, with cybercriminals becoming more sophisticated and exploiting new attack vectors. Staying informed about emerging threats and understanding their implications is crucial for effective cybersecurity management.

Building a Comprehensive Cybersecurity Strategy:

We discussed the steps involved in developing a comprehensive cybersecurity strategy. Conducting risk assessments, developing policies and procedures, training employees, and creating incident response plans are all critical components of a robust cybersecurity strategy. By following best practices and incorporating these elements into their organizational framework, non-technical executives can establish a strong security posture.

Compliance and Regulatory Considerations:

Compliance with cybersecurity standards and regulations is essential for organizations. Failure to comply can result in significant financial penalties and reputational damage. We discussed various regulations, such as the General Data Protection Regulation (GDPR) and the California Consumer Privacy Act

(CCPA), and emphasized the importance of staying up-to-date with changing regulations to maintain compliance.

Addressing Unique Challenges:

We explored the unique cybersecurity challenges presented by cloud-based applications, mobile devices, IoT devices, and remote work environments. Each of these areas requires specific security considerations and countermeasures. By understanding the risks associated with these technologies and implementing appropriate security measures, organizations can protect their data and systems.

The Role of Cybersecurity Insurance:

We discussed the importance of cybersecurity insurance as a means to mitigate financial losses and manage the impact of a cybersecurity incident. Cybersecurity insurance can provide coverage for costs related to data breaches, legal expenses, and reputational damage. Non-technical executives should carefully assess their organization's risk profile and consider obtaining cybersecurity insurance as part of their overall risk management strategy.

The Importance of Recruiting Cybersecurity Talent:

The demand for skilled cybersecurity professionals continues to outpace the available talent pool. We emphasized the
importance of recruiting and hiring qualified cybersecurity
personnel to strengthen an organization's security capabilities.
Identifying the necessary skills and experience, understanding
the roles and responsibilities within the cybersecurity team, and
implementing effective recruitment strategies are essential for
building a competent cybersecurity workforce.

Managing Third-Party Cybersecurity Risks:

Working with third-party vendors and partners introduces
additional cybersecurity risks. We discussed the importance
of assessing and managing these risks through effective vendor
management practices and due diligence. By implementing
comprehensive vendor security assessments and establishing
contractual obligations for cybersecurity, organizations can
reduce the potential for supply chain compromises.

Responding to Cybersecurity Incidents:

Despite best efforts, cybersecurity incidents may still occur. We
highlighted the importance of having an incident response plan
in place to detect, contain, and recover from incidents effectively. We discussed the steps involved in incident response,
such as incident reporting, investigation, containment, and
recovery, to minimize the impact of a cybersecurity breach.

106

Future Trends in Cybersecurity:

We explored the future trends in cybersecurity, including the impact of emerging technologies such as artificial intelligence, quantum computing, and 5G networks. These advancements bring both opportunities and challenges for cybersecurity. Staying ahead of the curve by understanding these trends and adapting security strategies accordingly is crucial for organizations to maintain a strong security posture.

In conclusion, cybersecurity is no longer just a technical concern. Non-technical executives play a critical role in ensuring the security and resilience of their organizations. By understanding the importance of cybersecurity, staying informed about evolving threats, and implementing a comprehensive cybersecurity strategy, non-technical executives can effectively protect their organizations from cyber threats and minimize the potential impact of cybersecurity incidents. We hope that this book has provided valuable insights and guidance to help non-technical executives navigate the complex world of cybersecurity and make informed decisions to safeguard their organizations in the digital age.

Glossary

- **Cybersecurity**: The practice of protecting computer systems, networks, and sensitive information from unauthorized access, theft, damage, or other malicious attacks.
- **Cyber attacks**: Malicious attempts to disrupt, damage, or gain unauthorized access to a computer system or network.
- **Cloud-based applications and services**: Software applications and services that are hosted on remote servers and accessed over the internet.
- **Mobile devices**: Portable electronic devices such as smartphones, tablets, and laptops that can connect to the internet and store sensitive information.
- **Internet of Things (IoT)**: A network of physical devices, vehicles, home appliances, and other objects that are embedded with sensors, software, and connectivity to exchange data over the internet.
- **Compliance with regulations**: Adhering to legal and regulatory requirements related to cybersecurity, such as data privacy laws and industry-specific regulations.
- **Cybersecurity insurance**: Insurance policies that provide coverage for costs related to data breaches, legal expenses, and reputational damage resulting from a cybersecurity incident.
- **Third-party risks**: Risks associated with vendors, suppli-

ers, contractors, or other third-party entities that have access to a company's sensitive information or systems.

- **Incidents**: Any event that compromises the confidentiality, integrity, or availability of a company's information or systems, such as a data breach or cyber attack.
- **Remote work environments**: Work environments where employees work from home or other remote locations, often using personal devices and accessing company systems over the internet.
- **IT** : Information Technology, refers to the use of computers, software, networks, and other digital technologies to process, store, and transmit information. IT encompasses a wide range of activities, including designing and developing software applications, managing computer networks and databases, providing technical support and troubleshooting, and ensuring the security and privacy of digital information.
- **Social engineering:** is a type of cyber attack that involves manipulating people into divulging sensitive information or performing actions that can compromise the security of computer systems or networks. Social engineering attacks typically exploit human emotions such as fear, curiosity, or trust to trick individuals into revealing passwords, clicking on malicious links, or downloading malware.
- **Exploit**: Piece of software or code that takes advantage of a vulnerability or weakness in a computer system or application to carry out a malicious action. Exploits can be used by cybercriminals to gain unauthorized access to systems, steal sensitive data, or cause damage to computer networks. Exploits can take many forms, including viruses, worms, Trojans, and other types of malware. Exploits can

be delivered through various attack vectors, such as email attachments, malicious websites, or network vulnerabilities.

- **Vulnerability**: refers to a weakness or flaw in a computer system, network, or application that can be exploited by cybercriminals to carry out malicious activities. Vulnerabilities can take many forms, such as software bugs, configuration errors, or design flaws.

- **Malware**: Software designed to harm or exploit computer systems, networks, or users. The term "malware" is short for "malicious software." Malware can take many forms, including viruses, worms, Trojans, ransomware, and spyware. Malware can be used by cybercriminals to gain unauthorized access to systems, steal sensitive data, or cause damage to computer networks. Malware can be delivered through various attack vectors, such as email attachments, malicious websites, or network vulnerabilities.

- **Firewall**: Network security system which monitors and controls incoming and outgoing network traffic based on predetermined security rules. The primary purpose of a firewall is to prevent unauthorized access to or from a private network.

- **Virtualization**: Technology which allows multiple operating systems or applications to run on a single physical computer or server. Virtualization creates a virtual environment that simulates the behavior of a physical computer, allowing multiple virtual machines (VMs) to run on a single physical machine. Each VM is isolated from the others and has its own virtual hardware, including CPU, memory, storage, and network interfaces. Virtualization enables organizations to consolidate their IT infrastructure, reduce hardware costs, and improve resource utilization. It also provides greater flexibility and scalability, allowing organizations to quickly provision and deprovision virtual machines as needed.

- **MFA**: Multi-Factor Authentication, security mechanism that requires users to provide two or more forms of authentication to access a system or application. MFA is designed to enhance the security of user accounts by adding an extra layer of protection against unauthorized access. The three common factors of authentication are:

1. Something you know (such as a password or PIN)

2. Something you have (such as a security token or smart card)

3. Something you are (such as a fingerprint or facial recognition)

By requiring users to provide two or more of these factors, MFA makes it more difficult for attackers to gain access to user accounts, even if they have obtained the user's password.

- **Firmware**: Software that is embedded in a hardware device, such as a computer motherboard, printer, or router. Firmware is designed to control the behavior of the hardware device and provide low-level control over its functions. Firmware is typically stored in non-volatile memory, such as ROM or flash memory, and is not easily modified by the user. Firmware updates are often released by the device manufacturer to fix bugs, add new features, or improve performance.

- **Software**: Type of computer program that is designed to perform specific tasks or functions on a computer or other electronic device. Software can be installed on a computer or device and can be easily modified or updated by the user. Examples of software include operating systems, applications, utilities, and games.

- **Bot**: short for "robot," is a type of software application that is designed to automate tasks that are typically performed by humans. Bots can be programmed to perform a wide range of tasks, from simple tasks like answering frequently asked questions to more complex tasks like analyzing data or interacting with other software applications.

- **Attack surface**: refers to the sum total of all the possible entry points or vulnerabilities in a system or network that an attacker can exploit to gain unauthorized access, steal data, or cause damage. The attack surface includes all the hardware, software, and network components that are exposed to potential threats, as well as the various interfaces and protocols that connect them.

  The attack surface can be expanded by various factors, such as the use of third-party software or services, the presence of unpatched vulnerabilities, or the lack of proper security controls. Attackers can use various techniques, such as social engineering, phishing, or malware, to exploit the vulnerabilities in the attack surface and gain access to sensitive data or systems.

- **DevSecOps**: is a software development approach that integrates security practices into the entire software development and deployment lifecycle. DevSecOps emphasizes the need for security to be an integral part of the software development process, rather than an afterthought or a separate activity.

  DevSecOps involves collaboration between development, security, and operations teams to ensure that security is built into every stage of the software development process.

This includes integrating security testing and analysis tools into the development pipeline, automating security processes, and continuously monitoring and assessing cloud-native environments.

About the Author

Raul Morales is a seasoned cybersecurity expert with a rich history in the field. With a career spanning over two decades, Raul has worked with leading tech companies. His expertise lies in a wide range of technologies, with a specific focus on mitigating cybersecurity threats, ensuring system availability, and aligning with global regulatory risk and compliance requirements.

Raul holds a Master's degree in Information and Systems Security from Cenfotec and a Bachelor's degree in Systems Engineering from Universidad Latina de Costa Rica. He is a Certified Information Systems Security Professional (CISSP) and a Certified Ethical Hacker, among other certifications.

Raul's passion for cybersecurity extends beyond his professional life. He is committed to educating professionals about the importance of cybersecurity, helping them navigate the digital landscape safely and effectively. The Present book aims to demystify the complex world of cybersecurity, making it accessible and understandable for everyone.

You can connect with me on:

🌐   https://www.linkedin.com/in/raul-morales-viquez/?locale=en_US